Contents

Acknowledgements

We are most grateful to all of the owners of these gardens for allowing us to photograph and describe them. Without their generous cooperation a book such as this could not be produced. We thank also the administrators of each site for making any special arrangements and for providing information for the text.

Dorothy Hunt Williams (Mrs. Wyatt A. Williams) deserves special thanks for allowing us to use her book HISTORIC VIRGINIA GARDENS (1975) as one of the resources for the essays and captions.

The cooperation of Donald Paulhus, designer, and James Patrick, publisher, Fort Church Press, was commendable. Together we made an efficient team.

Wendall Garrett's enthusiasm for Virginia history and her gardens is profound, and we appreciate his willingness to share it with us in the foreword. The legal guidance of Mr. Joseph C. Carter, Jr. facilitated the book's production.

Finally, we thank Joy Putman Favretti for her interest and advice in the preparation of the text.

The Authors and The Garden Club of Virginia.

Credits

© copyright 1993 by The Garden Club of Virginia

This book, or portions thereof, may not be reproduced in any manner without the written permission of The Garden Club of Virginia.

Library of Congress Catalog Card Number 93-71341
ISBN 1-881004-01-5

Edited by James B. Patrick

Designed by Donald G. Paulhus

Published by Fort Church Publishers, Inc.
Little Compton, RI 02837

Printed in Japan

*Gardens restored by The Garden Club of Virginia

GARDENS
&LANDSCAPES
of VIRGINIA

Photography by Richard Cheek
Text by Rudy J. Favretti

Sponsored by The Garden Club of Virginia
Published by Fort Church Publishers, Inc.

Preface

This book is a celebration of the richness and variety of the gardens that grace Virginia and an introduction to The Garden Club of Virginia's story of the restoration and preservation of the grounds and gardens surrounding the Commonwealth's historic landmarks.

When the first settlers arrived in the early seventeenth century they brought from England their custom of country houses and the gardens that naturally go with them. Arthur A. Shurcliff wrote in 1936: "The formal and spacious gardens, as well as the smaller ones, were copies of English gardens that the accumulating years had made perfect. The earliest gardens were built with painstaking care according to certain rules governing garden fashions developed in England."

Across Virginia today are old gardens fragrant with sweet smelling shrubs and velvety green with boxwood, and later gardens colorful with bulbs and native flowers in formal and informal arrangements that reflect the lifestyle of the owners.

Members of The Garden Club of Virginia believed that the picture of life in the past was not complete with the restoration of the buildings alone, but with the restoration of the grounds it became a vivid one. In 1929 this nine-year-old club rose to the challenge of restoring the grounds at Kenmore in Fredericksburg, the home of Colonel Fielding Lewis and his wife, Betty, only sister of George Washington. The challenge was seriously regarded, seriously undertaken, and seriously discharged, when members of The Garden Club of Virginia conceived of the idea of inviting friends to open their homes and gardens to the public for a small fee. The pilgrimage was unbelievably successful, and in the spring of 1993 The Garden Club of Virginia celebrated the sixtieth anniversary of Historic Garden Week. None of this would have been possible without the generosity of the owners of houses and gardens who graciously welcome our visitors each spring.

A native son and genius behind the camera, the talented Richard Cheek, has put on paper his vision of the glorious scenes of gardens in Virginia. Mr. Cheek's love of gardens comes naturally. His grandfather, the distinguished historian Dr. Douglas Southall Freeman, wrote: "These old gardens were very much in the life of the people of Virginia. It was the resort of the household from infancy to age. In some, the old glory survives. But in all of them the spirit of their founders still lives, very precious through the centuries, to hearten him who comes to visit them."

One of the most renowned landscape architects in America has written the text of this book. Rudy J. Favretti, professor emeritus of landscape architecture at the University of Connecticut, a Fellow of the American Society of Landscape Architects, and a specialist in landscape restoration and preservation, has served as a consultant on over five hundred historic sites. He is not only the landscape architect of The Garden Club of Virginia but also an Honorary Member and one of its most valued friends.

There is something magical on every page of this picture history of the gardens in Virginia. We hope you will experience the same joy, shared by all of us in The Garden Club of Virginia, that these historic gardens have been preserved for present and future generations.

Helen Turner Murphy

(Mrs. W. Tayloe Murphy, Jr.)
President, The Garden Club of Virginia

Foreword

In late April of the year 1607, three small vessels with 143 weary and storm-tossed travelers aboard entered Chesapeake Bay. In search of a suitable anchorage, the convoy slipped up the river they called the James, after their king; here on a peninsula, the vanguard of England's immigrants to this strange new land had reached their destination – Virginia, named in honor of England's Virgin Queen.

While the mortality rate for English people in the New World continued for decades to be appallingly high, by the late 1640s the population figures began showing a notable increase by heavy immigration. These men built small cottages for their homes and, as their prosperity increased, added to them or replaced them with larger farmhouses. Though they grew foodstuffs for their tables, they concentrated their efforts upon the intensive development of profitable tobacco, not only because it became their most valuable export crop but because it was the medium of exchange. By 1635 the population of the colony was just under five thousand. The Virginia frontier was being pushed forward into the wilderness, and into the forest clearings, and "the joviall weed," the "bewitching vegetable," the "esteemed weed," and the "chopping herbe of hell" – as tobacco was variously known – served as the basis for the colony's economic viability.

In 1642 there came to Virginia Sir William Berkeley – scholar, talented playwright, a magnetic personality, and member of a distinguished England family – who for much of the next thirty-five years would dominate the colony as a popular and successful governor. The colony he found when he arrived consisted of some 15,000 white people and 300 black slaves. He encouraged crop diversification and set a good example himself by planting flax, cotton, and rice, as well as experimenting with silkworm culture. But in spite of his best efforts tobacco plantations constituted the economic lifeblood of the colony and Virginia developed a one-crop economy. In 1671 Berkeley made the statement on cultural interests and schools in the colony for which he is best known, when declared: "I thank God there are no free schools nor printing, and I hope we shall not have [for a] hundred years; for learning has brought disobedience, and heresy and sects into the world, and printing has divulged them, and libels against the best government. God keep us from both!" Even though the General Assembly passed an act in 1661 creating a free school and a college, for one reason or another there were no tangible results until 1693 when the college finally became a reality, with the establishment of the College of William and Mary.

With the Restoration of the monarchy of Charles II in 1660, the loyalty of the Virginians to the Stuart side earned them their king's gratitude for which he raised the colony to the status of a dominion. Henceforth, Virginia was to be known as the Old Dominion. With the Glorious Revolution of 1688 and the accession of King William and Queen Mary, the newly crowned monarchs exhibited a genuine concern for the well-being of the Virginia people. The arrival of Captain Francis Nicholson in the colony as lieutenant governor, a competent executive, was simultaneous with an upturn in the colony's fortunes: settlements were spreading into the interior and Indian warfare was becoming less rampant. There was scientific progress on a modest scale. The Reverend John Clayton, and Anglican clergyman who spent two years at Jamestown in the 1680s, was a pioneering observer of soils, climate, and medicine. A contemporary, John Banister, who spent a decade and a half in the Old Dominion, was an eminent botanist. A later John Clayton, related to the other, who employed the leisure of a sinecure clerkship in Gloucester County to plant a botanical garden and assemble the herbarium speci-

mens, sent them to J.F. Gronovius of Leyden who systematized and described them in *Flora Virginica* (1743, 1762), a work regarded highly by Thomas Jefferson and Benjamin Franklin. More important than these scientists, who acquired their initial impulse in England where they were born, were native-born amateur scientists: John Custis of Williamsburg who carried on an extensive correspondence about seeds and plants with the famous Peter Collinson of London from 1734 and 1746; John Mitchell, a practicing physician in Middlesex County, whose contributions to botany, zoology, medicine, and map making were exceptional. Mitchell brought out his *Map of the British and French Dominions in North America* in London in 1755, which immediately became the standard. It saw seventeen reprints in four countries, and was complimented by being widely plagiarized before 1776. William Byrd II and Isham Randolph were others among Peter Collinson's "Brothers of the Spade." In 1763, while he was a student in medicine at the University of Edinburgh, Arthur Lee of Virginia was awarded Dr. John Hope's gold medal for promoting botany. When in 1698 the statehouse at Jamestown burned to the ground, the capital was moved to Middle Plantation by the General Assembly, and was renamed Williamsburg where it was to remain the colonial capital until the American Revolution. For eighty years Williamsburg was the place where the great Virginians of the colonial period gathered.

Few cities in America can point to a more scintillating galaxy of learned and cultivated men than those who trod the streets of this little town. The Reverend Hugh Jones wrote concerning the people of Williamsburg in *The Present State of Virginia* (1724): "They live in the same neat manner, dress after the same modes, and behave themselves exactly as the gentry in London; most families of any note having a coach, chariot, berlin or chaise." Professor William Small might reveal the wonders

of nature at the College, and another venerated teacher George Wythe peer through his new microscope, but Tidewater planters were no votaries of science, which, as Jefferson was to remark, demanded a "patient pursuit of facts and cautious combination and comparison of them" – a drudgery for which few of them had either the time or the taste. In 1773 when Josiah Quincy of Boston was making a survey of the colonies, he described the Virginia gentlemen, for whom "the ingenuity of a Locke or the discoveries of a Newton were considered as infinitely inferior to the accomplishments of him who knew when to shoulder a blind cock or to start a fleet horse . . . a spirit of inquiry and literature . . . is manifestly subordinate to a spirit of gaming, horse-racing and jockeying of all kinds . . . It is really affecting to consider what a prodigious number of men have not the least spark of taste, have no relish for the fine arts." This was a working gentry who valued practical learning, who led a gracious but not an intellectual life. The genius of this people lay in agriculture and politics, and displayed itself to the world as *noblesse oblige*, gracious hospitality, zest for living, and effortless courtesy.

Until 1820 Virginia had the largest population in the Union, but in that year it fell to second place, and by 1860 it had slipped to fifth. Virginians continue to live the simple, rural, pastoral life they adopted more than a century earlier, sharing only marginally in the increase of industry and trade that took place in the states to the north and west.

Rural Virginia – the Mother of Presidents – was the founder and keeper of Southern traditions. In the nineteenth century the vast majority of black and white Virginians still lived in the country on farms, large and small. There were no cities in the modern sense: Richmond in 1860 had under 38,000 inhabitants, while Norfolk, the next largest, had fewer than 15,000. Norfolk was recovering

from its destruction in the Revolution when La Rochefoucauld-Liancourt described it in 1796 as "one of the ugliest, most irregular, dirtiest towns that I have ever seen." Yet Norfolk, like Richmond, in the new nation was experiencing a substantial boom now that products from the interior were being shipped down the James River, and then on to Norfolk in the growing ocean trade. Mrs. Anne Royall, who visited Norfolk in 1828, wrote in her account of her journeys: " I expected to see an old, dirty-looking, clownish town. On the contrary...the houses are large and elegant, and many of them are surrounded by beautiful trees...The streets are well paved, lighted, and the neatest kept in any town in the Union except Providence." Virginia hospitality continued to be a salient characteristic. Henry Barnard of New England toured Virginia in 1833 and wrote: "You would delight in this region, merely to observe the difference in manners and habits, and to experience the princely hospitality of the gentle-born families." Nearly all roads were unspeakably bad and homes were widely separated; farmers might live miles from the nearest neighbors and seemed "to drop their full-dress and constrained townhabits, and live a free, rustic, shooting-jacket life," a northern traveler reported. Thanks to the ingenuity and leadership of several individuals and the various innovations, such as the introduction of gypsum and fertilizers and the organization of agricultural societies to promote their use, soil exhaustion and erosion of worn-out lands were checked, and by 1850 there was a distinct upturn in the general level of farming. Diversification of crops and the raising of livestock for sale were also important factors in the rise of Virginia farming before the Civil War. Truck crops were raised in the lower Tidewater and fruit orchards planted in the Piedmont and the Shenandoah Valley for export to the North. The growing of grain reached such proportions that, except for tobacco,

it eventually became Virginia's chief source of farm income. During the 1840s and 1850s colonies of Yankee farmers from the North came down and settled in the Tidewater counties, and relied on scientific techniques, crop rotation, and free labor to produce vegetables in great variety and abundance.

Virginia was a pastoral society with a provincial culture, and these transplanted Englishmen looked back to the mother country for cultural ideas – including gardening. A custom developed among wealthy Southerners of sending or taking their young men to Britain for advanced liberal or professional education. The creation of gardens in the New World, as well as the Old, was determined by intellectual, social, economic, political, and artistic forces, which in turn were mirrored in gardens: like architectural and furniture styles, gardens followed stylistic preferences of their time and place.

It was the rejection of the formality in gardens, where enclosing walls would vanish, that initiated the English landscape garden movement as we know it today with its less contrived scenery and natural imagery, with its exaggeratedly serpentine lines of walks on hillsides and around lakes. The theories and practical proposals for rural gardening were advocated by Richard Bradley in *Survey of the Ancient Husbandry and Gardening* (1725), where he recommended that a country seat be set "not amongst Enclosures, but in a champaign, open Country." These ideas about the English garden had support from both literature and painting. In fact, the contributions of other arts to gardens were enormously vital: as Walpole would put it, "Poetry, Painting and Gardening, or the science of Landscape, will forever by men of Taste be deemed Three Sisters, or the *Three New Graces* who dress and adorn nature." The most decisive literary influence was from classical Roman writings about rural life and the virtuous man. Englishmen who had been on the Grand Tour thus

translated to the northern climate of the British Isles what they knew of Italian Renaissance garden forms, adapting the Roman villa-farm to the English weather, topography, and society. One of the characteristic claims of English landscape gardeners was that their gardens were opened by extensive vistas across the ha-ha into the distant, often agricultural, countryside: what Alexander Pope termed "calling in the country." The admired feature of Italian Renaissance gardens of water, groves, distant hills, ruins, bridges, and trees was recalled in Walpole's account of William Kent: "he leaped the fence, and saw that all nature was a garden." Gardens were envisioned as picturesque history paintings, as design settings or conversation pieces, where human visitors were both actors and spectators, identifying themselves with classical culture.

Although the landscape garden was an English creation, it became an international style, copied extensively, particularly in Virginia at Mount Vernon, Monticello, and many other great Virginia historic sites. The largest slaveholder in antebellum Virginia was Samuel Hairston, "whose gardens at his homestead in Henry County were likened to Paradise." Paradise, Arcadia, Elysium – here there is the subtle implication of transition and change, from the fragmentation of Jeffersonian Enlightenment values of harmony, balance, restraint, and the distancing of emotion, to the congruence of inward and outward, a transition of emphasis from the public to the private sphere, the development of creative transactions between the individualism of man and the divinity in nature, central to the Romantic imagination. While Romanticism in the North catered to change, Southern Romanticism was more static and reactionary, especially following the Virginia Convention of 1831-32, that was followed by a rigid proslavery conservatism. Nourished on the pasto-

ral primitivism of Jean-Jacques Rousseau and the medieval romances of Sir Walter Scott, the literary genres that flourished in the Old South during the age of Romanticism were given over to the cult of sentiment and reflective sadness and alienation: with the emphasis on the authenticity of the emotions, a new significance was given to autobiography, the psychological novel, the self-scrutinizing poem, and the historicist narrative. The predominant tone of Romanticism in antebellum Virginia was melancholy, which may explain the susceptibility of Virginians to the Cavalier myth and the enduring legend of the Lost Cause following the Civl War.

In the swift-paced confusion and frantic bustle of contemporary American life, there still exists the Virginia ideal of the good life, which is reflected in her gardens as this volume so amply demonstrates: the community of grace, self-respect, pride, gentleness, honor, and hospitality; of men and women who know what they want to be, and who love the place they inhabit. What Robert Beverley wrote about Virginians nearly three hundred years ago still applies: "The clearness and brightness of the sky add new vigor to their spirits and perfectly remove all sullen and splenetic thoughts. Here they enjoy all the benefits of a warm sun, and by their shady groves are protected from its inconvenience. Here their senses are entertained with an endless succession of native pleasures. Their eyes are ravaged with the beauties of naked nature. Their ears are serenaded with the perpetual murmur of brooks and the thorough bass which the wind plays when it wantons through the trees. The merry birds, too, join their pleasing notes to this rural consort, especially the mock [ing] birds, who love society so well that whenever they see mankind they will perch upon a twig very near them and sing the sweetest wild airs in the world."

Wendell Garrett
Senior Vice-President
AMERICAN DECORATIVE ARTS
SOTHEBY'S, NEW YORK

Introduction

All of Virginia is a garden. Her rolling terrain from the Tidewater to the Blue Ridge mountains, her villages and cities that grew along her waterways, and her jewel-like gardens throughout the Commonwealth, are the scenes that artists paint and visitors come to see.

Virginians are fortunate to have a long history in the stewardship of her gardens, and other Americans benefit as well. The Mount Vernon Ladies Association became stewards of MOUNT VERNON in 1856. A third of a century later, The Association for the Preservation of Virginia Antiquities was formed, and they soon began acquiring properties of which they now have twenty-eight. Colonial Williamsburg started its garden restoration program in the late 1920s.

In 1920, The Garden Club of Virginia was founded. Nine years later, in 1929, its first restoration, KENMORE, was begun. After the restoration of both KENMORE and STRATFORD, Historic Garden Week was started in 1933, as a way to raise funds for the restoration of many more gardens, a list totalling over thirty-three sites with forty-five separate gardens.

Gardens and landscapes restored by The Garden Club of Virginia fall into several general categories. There are those that are true restorations because there is sufficient research data on which to base a restoration plan. Examples of those are BACON'S CASTLE, CARLYLE HOUSE, GRACE ARENTS' GARDEN, MONTICELLO and PREST-WOULD. In other instances, there is insufficient data on which to base these decisions in which case an appropriate landscape setting for the period of the building is installed at the request of the owner. BURWELL-MORGAN MILL, KERR PLACE, POINT-OF-HONOR, PORTSMOUTH COURTHOUSE, SCOTCHTOWN, SMITHFIELD PLANTATION, SMITH'S FORT, ADAM THOR-OUGHGOOD HOUSE, WOODROW WILSON BIRTHPLACE, and WILTON are examples of this category.

In other instances, research data do not offer details for a known garden so it is developed conjecturally as at CENTER HILL, GUNSTON HALL, KENMORE, STRATFORD HALL, and THE UNIVERSITY OF VIRGINIA. Many times it is not possible to restore the original landscape even if there is reliable documentation. In these cases, appropriate settings are created based on the period of the project, such as at CHRIST CHURCH, LANCASTER, and THE MEWS in Richmond. Sometimes The Garden Club of Virginia is asked to restore a feature in the landscape such as the wood-capped forcing wall at OATLANDS.

Whatever the category, the work of The Garden Club of Virginia in the restoration of gardens and landscapes is unique in the nation. No other volunteer organization has consistently raised funds for a span of more than sixty years to restore so many important landscapes. It is fitting that, of all the states in the nation, this should happen in the Commonwealth of Virginia because she is so rich in important gardens of all periods.

Virginia's restored gardens have become models throughout the nation. This book is a celebration of over sixty years of garden restoration by The Garden Club of Virginia, and the effort that Virginians have made to preserve their important landscapes. It is not a history but rather a compendium of the gardens that The Garden Club of Virginia has restored, as well as other gardens open to the public on a regular basis.

On page 2 is an alphabetical listing of the gardens included in this book. The designers of the gardens, when known, follow each listing. The Garden Club of Virginia restorations are marked with an asterisk.

Rudy J. Favretti
Landscape Architect
The Garden Club of Virginia

Giving order to wilderness and enclosing these organized spaces against the ravages of man and beast were major concerns of Virginia's earliest planters. At BACON'S CASTLE,

careful archaeological research revealed a series of yards and gardens, among them a forecourt in front of the house as well as a large garden to one side (figure 1). This garden, the best documented for the seventeenth in this country, was larger than a modern football field.

On the north end of the Allen family's large garden was a brick forcing wall and studies reveal the other sides were probably enclosed by hedges (figures 2,3). Within this enclosure was a grid of walks. On either side of the twelve feet wide central walk were three garden plots, each separated from the other by cross-walks. Within these garden plots, row vegetables were grown to feed Arthur Allen's family and servants (figure 1).

Between the outer walks and the enclosing hedges were six feet wide border beds that ran the length of the garden on both sides and along the south end. In these beds were grown small-scale crops such as herbs, bush fruits, and flowers (figure 2). In front of the forcing wall was a deeper bed of twenty feet where early crops were planted, tender plants propagated, and fruit trees were grown against the wall to gain the solar heat in cool seasons.

The hedges installed as part of the recreated garden at BACON'S CASTLE are Mockorange, (Philadelphus coronarius). While Hawthorn (Crataegus) would have been a likely choice, it was rejected because of its susceptability to insects and diseases. John Gerard, in his HERBAL (1633), documents the use of Mockorange as a hedge plant, and at this time it is pest free (figure 3).

There were other features in the garden as well. At the east end of the most northerly cross-walk archaeology discovered the foundation of a garden house or office about twenty by thirty-six feet in size, while at the end of each cross-walk on the west side of the garden were sitting areas.

High maintenance costs precluded the restoration of all six vegetable plots at BACON'S CASTLE. Only two of them were recreated, and the other four were planted with grass (figure 1).

The garden at the ADAM THOROUGHGOOD HOUSE (figures 4-8) is conjectural because research data was lacking at the time of its installation. It is apparent that Alden Hopkins, its twentieth-century designer, received his inspiration from sketches which were published in Thomas Hill's THE GARDENER'S LABYRINTH (1577), the first popular book on gardening published in the English language.

The ADAM THOROUGHGOOD garden consists of two large compartmentalized plots on either side of a central walk, a traditional English layout for the seventeenth century and one copied in this country. Along the central walk are rails or low fences on which are grown espaliered fruit trees. On the outer boundaries of the garden, as termini to the cross-walk, are two large arbors.

Prior to the early eighteenth century in England, gardens were tightly enclosed spaces. From within the arrangement gave a sense of confinement and focus upon the interior. In some instances, mounds or mounts were built for looking over the garden wall, but these were not common.

Larkspurs in the border bed. BACON'S CASTLE.

BACON'S CASTLE (1665) (figure 1). An aerial view of the recreated garden and unrestored forecourt.

Figure 2. The brick forcing wall which protects the north starting beds.

Figure 3. BACON'S CASTLE border beds contain a mixture of flowers, herbs, and fruits. A Mockorange hedge defines the outer edge of the garden.

5

6

7

ADAM THOROUGHGOOD HOUSE (c. 1680), is shown in figure 4. Clipped hedges, topiary, espaliered fruit trees, and sparsely planted flowers are characteristic of seventeenth century English gardens (figures 5, 6, and 7). For ornament, a popular sculpture of the period was a carved animal displayed on a pedestal, or an ornamented finial on a post of the inner fence surrounding the garden beds (figure 6).

8

Previous pages 18-19: Arbors were important features in medieval and Tudor England, and they have continued to adorn gardens since. They provided support for climbing plants, both utilitarian and ornamental, as well as shade for outdoor activities. The ADAM THOROUGH-GOOD garden has two arbors, one at each end of the cross-walk.

LYNNHAVEN (c. 1724) (figure 8), while architecturally reminiscent of the seventeenth century, has been dated through dendrochronology of its structural beams to the early eighteenth century. The landscape is not based on documentary evidence but contains elements – the paling fence, the well-head, and herbs – which are characteristic of its date of construction.

Rivers were a natural system for travel and transport in eighteenth century Virginia. When roads were muddy and rutted, the rivers offered smooth access to commercial centers

from plantations and other settlements.

As plantations were built along Virginia's many rivers, careful thought went into their planning. House, land, and river were integrated into a workable whole which was then made beautiful by the addition of trees, lawns, and gardens. The river itself became a borrowed landscape or a visual extension of the garden, a concept that had been employed in ancient times and had been revived during the Italian Renaissance, especially by Palladio in the villa gardens built before 1580.

The basic plan was a long central walk or allee on axis with an extension of the central hallway of the house. At the far end of the walk was a view of the river and beyond. Visitors could arrive by land, where they would drive or walk into a landscaped forecourt and then enter the house. They could also arrive by water and approach the house through the garden. This river plantation layout prevailed in the eighteenth century, not only in Virginia, but in other southern states as well (figure 1, page 22).

On either side of the central garden walk were garden plots within a grid of walks, similar to the arrangement used at BACON'S CASTLE. However, around each plot was a border bed planted with flowers and shurbs to shield the vegetables, which grew in the center, from view. Each side of the main walk mirrored the other so that the garden was symmetrical. This ancient style of garden design began to change in early eighteenth century England, but it took the better part of that century before the new style was adopted here.

It is this style of garden that we associate with BERKELEY, BRANDON, CARTER'S GROVE, and WESTOVER. SHIRLEY, another James River Plantation, had a similar layout.

Site and personal taste obviously affected the garden's location. At PRESTWOULD PLANTATION, the garden was placed at one side of the house while a strong vista alone united the hallway with the Roanoke River over undulating and sloping terrain. At STRATFORD HALL, the two gardens extend the hallway of the mansion, but the hall was not on axis with the Potomac River. Here, too, the link between house and river is visual, not physical.

Finally, at GUNSTON HALL, another variation exists. Here the garden axis walk extends the hallway of the house, and while the river can be seen from the walk, it is some distance away across a vast deer park. Again, the connection between river and house is visual.

The visual inclusion of a distant view into the garden was an attempt to borrow from the beauties of nature. At BERKELEY, BRANDON, WESTOVER, and CARTER'S GROVE it was the James River. At GUNSTON HALL, though water could be seen in the far distance, the deer park was most evident. At PRESTWOULD, undulating terrain intervened between the house and river.

Including a distant view as an extension of the garden became an important concept in landscape planning in the eighteenth century. It is a basic concept in the design of gardens today, though the practice has become difficult because of unsightly intrusions in the line of vision.

Pan playing his silent seranade. BRANDON.

1

BRANDON (c. 1765) (figure 1). The central walk which leads from the mansion to the James River is terminated by a mound on which sits a large urn with the River as background. Border beds along the walk once enclosed vegetable plots between a grid of walks.

Figure 2. The land front of BRANDON, a Palladian style house with a central block flanked by wings which contained the household services. Groves of trees shade the house while rows of them define the garden's boundaries (figure 4).

Figure 3. Small buildings, built as tool or necessary houses, were prominent in Virginia gardens.

Overleaf, pages 24, 25: The magnificent BRANDON urn silhouetted against the James River at sunrise.

2

3

4

WESTOVER (c. 1730), built by William E. Byrd II, has had many alterations since. It is believed that the basic garden plan is original to the eighteenth century with its symmetrical arrangements of garden beds within a grid of walks. It has the long and wide central allee leading from the mansion to the James River. Some narrower walks cross, and others parallel, the central axis thus creating an elaborate grid. The intervening garden plots were once devoted to vegetables and the outer border was planted with herbs, flowers, and small fruits (figure 5).

Most Virginia plantations had private family graveyards, which were part of the garden, usually terminating a cross-walk. William E. Byrd II's monument is a prominent feature in the garden at WESTOVER (figure 6).

The land front of WESTOVER with its characteristic tree canopy and large forecourt (figure 7).

BERKELEY (1726), was the seat of the Harrison family. The mansion was built by Benjamin Harrison IV, and the garden layout is presumed to be original. BERKELEY was the home of the ninth and twenty-third presidents.

Figure 8 shows the uppermost cross-walk of the traditional garden edged with boxwood. Until the early nineteenth century, boxwood was used as accent in Virginia gardens, and after that time there was a revival of parterre gardening associated with the Renaissance.

Figure 9. The terraced ground at BERKELEY which lends majesty to the garden.

11

12

CARTER'S GROVE, a Colonial Williamsburg property, sits on 522 acres of the original plantation with an elegant prospect of the James River. In the mid-1970's archaeological research was conducted which revealed the exact layout of the original garden on axis with the central hall of the mansion. The garden is a traditional eight plot grid plan enclosed by a paling fence (figure 11).

Figure 10. CARTER'S GROVE (c. 1750). The water front in mid-summer with a Crape Myrtle (Lagerstroemia indica) in bloom.

Topiaries were added when CARTER'S GROVE was landscaped in the colonial revival manner earlier in this century (figure 12).

Overleaf, pages 32, 33: The Red Cedar (Juniperus virginiana), grows from Canada to Florida, and west to the Rocky Mountains. In Virginia it grows luxuriantly; hence, it has been used in allees to delineate drives since the eighteenth century. This magnificent planting is along the driveway at CARTER'S GROVE.

PRESTWOULD PLANTATION (1795) (figure 13). Lady Jean Skipwith designed this grid plan garden in about 1796. On the west side it is surrounded by semi-circular beds, called "horseshoe beds", where plants she wished to study were grown. The garden includes an octagonal summer house at its south end (figure 14). In the upper left, figure 13, are some earliest known examples of slave quarters in this country.

Figure 15. From the parlor, seated at Lady Jean Skipwith's writing table, one can view a Banskia Rose (Rosa Banksiae) tumbling over the garden's main entrance arbor. In the foreground are some of her letters and books. Her vasculum, filled with plant specimens, sits at the window.

Figure 16. Lady Jean Skipwith's tomb lies in the small family graveyard which is also a sanctuary for old roses.

Figures 17, 18. These gates have been restored from the originals considered to be the earliest extant examples of eighteenth century garden gates in the country.

Overleaf, pages 38, 39: This hunt scene wallpaper in PRESTWOULD'S dining room was entitled LA CHASSE DE CAMPIGN by its manufacturers, Jacquemart et Denard, 1814. It was installed at PRESTWOULD in 1831.

GUNSTON HALL (1755) (figure 21). George Mason's mansion seen through a Weeping Cherry planted in this century.

Figure 22. Flowering Quince (Chaenomeles speciosa) combine with daffodils to provide a vibrant setting for one of the two belvederes.

Overleaf, pages 42, 43: The top and largest level of the GUNSTON HALL garden. Much of the boxwood is original.

25

26

GUNSTON, once a plantation of vast acreage, consisted of a series of fields, pastures and cropland. This flock of sheep (figure 25) reminds us of the diversity of agriculture that once existed beyond the edges of the garden.

Figure 24. The path to the GUNSTON graveyard is canopied by an allee of solemn Red Cedars (Juniperus virginiana).

There were two belvederes or lookout points on each side of the garden as well as the one in the center described above. On these side belvederes, landscape architect Alden Hopkins designed summerhouses with gothic details repeating those found in the mansion's porch (figure 26).

STRATFORD HALL (late 1730's) (figure 30). Thomas Lee built this great hall. His great-grandson, General Robert E. Lee, was born here in 1807.

Figure 28. Purely functional features such as a mill pond also served as aesthetic elements in the landscape.

Figures 27, 29. The armillary sphere which is the central focal point in the East Garden.

Overleaf, pages 48, 49: The cliffs overlooking the Potomac at STRATFORD are a significant part of the natural landscape.

33

34

Figure 32. An aerial view of the East Garden at STRATFORD.
Eighteenth century gardeners rarely considered placing a garden on sloping ground without terracing it first. The STRATFORD HALL garden has four terraces that fall away from the mansion's east end. While each garden plot between the walkway grid is now treated as an ornamental parterre, these beds were probably devoted to a variety of plants in the eighteenth century including vegetables, herbs, and bush fruits as well as flowers and shrubs (figure 32).

STRATFORD HALL commands a serene prospect over the gently rolling fields to the Potomac River. Figure 33.

Virginia plantations were complex entities of which gardens were just one part. Most of them were over one thousand acres, and many contained as much as five thousand or more.

At the expense of over-simplification, we may think of these plantations as concentric zones with the center being the household and gardens. The next zone held the barns, stables, and associated yards, and beyond these were the pastures for grazing animals, and fields for growing hay, grains, and large scale crops such as tobacco. Then came the forests which provided wood for fuel and timber.

One must not think of these zones as perfect concentric circles. This simple zone arrangement was affected by the topography of the land, the nature of the soil, and locations of ledges, rock outcroppings, streams, and other natural features. Where land was poor and rocky, for example, a forests would be left upon it even though it was within a "zone" of pasture. These natural features varied from plantation to plantation making each one different.

The landscaped grounds surrounding the house were, in most cases, the smallest acreage of all the many use zones of the plantation. Kitchen gardens were generally much larger than flower gardens because of the needs of the large family as well as the many servants. All vegetables, ranging from staples such as potatoes and beans to "extras" such as lettuce and herbs, had to be grown on the site. Fruits, too, from the bush types to large apple, pear, and cherry trees occupied much land since fifty trees required as much as an acre or more of land.

Most of the land on Virginia plantations was taken up with pastures and fields as well as forests. The concept of ammending soils with fertilizer and lime materials to produce higher yields had not yet come into common practice; hence, it required vast areas to grow grass for pasturing and hay and grains to store for winter feed.

Virginia's early planters were keenly aware of nature and what it offered. Houses were sited where they had the best prospect, where they would be well above the water table, and had the advantage of the summer breezes. Gardens were situated to capture the late winter and early spring sun and yet not be parched during the hot summer heat. Barns were placed away from the houses and out of the path of prevailing breezes. The poorest land was left in forest while the best was turned into productive fields.

As plantations were established a pattern grew on the land. This pattern was defined by fences that separated the gardens, pastures, and fields, and the whole was laced together by paths and roads for access.

This careful order prevailed on most eighteenth century plantations with variation based on conditions. Each owner placed his mark on the layout by adding products of his own taste. Some had long tree-lined allees, as straight as a die, approaching the front forecourt of the house. Others planned winding approach roads. Some of the gardens were ornamented with sundials and sculpture, while others were unadorned. The plants grown on some plantations were purely utilitarian while others included a good supply of ornamentals. The work of the plantation and the configuration of the land dictated its various parts.

A glimpse at the garden through its gate, KENMORE.

KENMORE (1752). Only three of the original 860 acres on which Fielding and Betty Washington Lewis built their mansion remain. KENMORE was built upon a commanding ridge overlooking a large garden which extended far beyond the present walls. Fields of hay and grain reached out in all directions beyond the garden. In figure 1 above, the white pavilion (copied from that at Federal Hill, Fredericksburg) is one of two from which visitors may sit and look out over the entire garden including the Katherine Hayes memorial Garden shown in the foreground. A large Yellowood (Cladratis lutea) shades the north pavilion and upper garden terrace. In late spring it offers an abundance of white bloom and throughout the year its sculptural trunk enhances the garden (figure 2).

WOODLAWN (1805) (figure 3). On February 22, 1799, Eleanor Parke (Nelly) Custis, grand-daughter of Martha Custis Washington, married Lawrence Lewis, son of Fielding and Betty Lewis of KENMORE. As a gift George Washington deeded to them two thousand acres on which they built WOODLAWN.

The mansion sits high on a hill commanding dramatic views. As was the custom of the day, groves surrounded the mansion, hence the name WOODLAWN.

In letters written to friends, Nelly Custis mentioned the roses, woodbine, flowering shrubs, dogwoods, pines, cedars and fruits and vegetables that she planted in her garden. Landscape architect, Alden Hopkins, included these original plants within the compartmented garden. His west lawn design is reminiscent of the bowling green at MOUNT VERNON, or the west lawn at MONTICELLO, surrounded as it is with a meandering walk and shrubberies.

A long allee of Golden Raintrees (Koelreuteria paniculata) divides the large garden at WOODLAWN (figure 4). Beneath them are borders of flowers and herbs to visually enrich the walk and to screen the vegetable plots that would have existed beyond. These flowers are often cut and brought into the mansion to enhance the elegant Federal interior (figure 5).

Many of the ancient trees at WOODLAWN date from the nineteenth century including this magnificent Camperdown Elm (Ulmus camperdownii), planted at a time when sculptural trees, especially weeping ones, were very popular (figure 6).

7

WILTON (1753). William Randolph III and his wife
Ann Carter Harrison had this mansion built on a site
six miles east of its present location. In 1933, it was
moved and saved from destruction by the National
Society of Colonial Dames of the Commonwealth of
Virginia (figure 8). Today, WILTON sits in a grove with
fine vistas to the James River (figures 7, 9).

KERR PLACE (1799) (figure 10). John S. Ker, as the
name was spelled then, built this fine house on 364
acres of land in what is now Onancock, on Virginia's
Eastern Shore. When John S. Ker died his son John
inherited KERR PLACE, and in 1826 John left it to his
friend, George S. Snead. When Snead sold it in 1876,
only seven acres of land were sold with it.

Although archaeology has not revealed a garden
within the present acerage, it seems certain that, in
the fashion of the times, KERR PLACE stood in a
grove of towering trees. Today a simple Crape Myrtle
(Lagerstroemia indica) allee traverses the rear lawn.
A peek through the circular window in the mansion's
roof pediment provides a charming glimpse of the allee
which is terminated by a grape arbor (figures 10, 11).

EYRE HALL (1735) (figure 14). This property was acquired by John Thomas and Daniel Eyre in 1662 from William Berkeley. Since that time descendents of Eyre have been its stewards. While the main house was built in 1735, additions were made in 1760, and today the magnificent house sits on the south side of a very large, traditionally eighteenth century garden.

On the square Dairy Building at the far right one can see rare examples of shaped-slat air vents, and a plaster cove cornice. Crape Myrtles (Lagerstoemia indica) enclose the long entrance drive leading to EYRE HALL, (figure 12). This tree was introduced to America from China in 1747, and since that time, has enlivened the hot, dry days of early August in Virginia. From the shade of the porch one can enjoy more Crape Myrtles which are featured in the garden as well (figure 13).

On the west side of the old garden sit the ruins of a very early orangery. In the center of these ruins is a spinal wall that contained three fireplaces. Heat from fires circulated through concealed ducts within the wall to heat the glass-enclosed structure (figure 15).

At the end of one of the cross-walks in the garden is the family graveyard. The orangery can be seen in the background (figure 16).

ASH LAWN (1799). James Monroe, at the encouragement of Thomas Jefferson, purchased one thousand acres near MONTICELLO. On this land he built a small house, later enlarged, and here he and Mrs. Monroe lived for about twenty years prior to his becoming fifth president of the United States (figure 19).

Figure 17. Informal flower gardens surround the lawn adjacent to the house at ASH LAWN. These gardens underscore impressive vistas to the surrounding mountains.

Today a large boxwood garden, in which stands a statue of President Monroe, graces the estate (figure 18).

Did all residences in Virginia have gardens in the eighteenth century and before? This is a common question on restoration sites, especially when careful intensive research yields no answers.

It is safe to assume that most of them did. The first United States Census, taken in 1790, informs us that well over ninety percent of the population was engaged in farming. When there were few stores and markets to sell fresh produce, almost everyone, including doctors, lawyers, and craftsmen, had gardens.

Were these gardens strictly utilitarian or were there ornamental ones as well, or perhaps a combination? Utility, no doubt, was given first priority. Ornamentation would depend upon the amount of time the owners, or servants, had to devote to the garden. The desire of the owners to have flowers would also influence the decision.

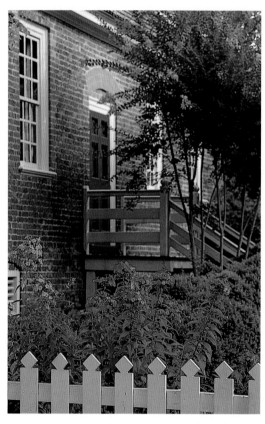

With houses built on the fringes of settlements or on the frontier, such as SMITH-FIELD PLANTATION (pages 70,71), there is the tendency to think that the hardships encountered there would preclude anything other than utilitarian gardens. However, there are accounts, such as the following, written by Baron Ludwig von Closen in 1782 after a visit to SCOTCHTOWN. "The grounds at Scotchtown are very pretty and there are little woods in the shade of which we took country walks. The garden is an attractive sight. There are several pretty flower-beds although these are still rather neglected in this country."

There were three major categories of structures associated with the eighteenth century plantation which greatly influenced and gave dimension to the landscape. The first category included outbuildings and dependencies, such as necessaries, smokehouses, washhouses, servants' quarters, plantation offices, milk houses, barns, sheds, and related structures. Also in this group would be small shops or "manufactures" such as the blacksmith's shop, the cooperage, and similar shops. These were placed in a particular order based on their functional relationship to one another and to the main house.

Mills, which were necessary for sustaining life in the eighteenth century, made up the second category of structures affecting the plantation landscape. These included saw mills and grist mills. These mills were sited next to water, their source of power. Many mills were privately owned and served the plantation only. Others, such as the BURWELL-MORGAN MILL, were located at cross-roads for the benefit of all.

The third category of structures that gave dimension to the landscape was the fencing. Those fences enclosing gardens were often palings, nailed so close together as to exclude even the smallest form of wildlife, or they might have been walls of stone or brick. Field and pasture fences were of rails, the worm or Virginia rail fence being a common type.

Hedges, though apparently planted to enclose gardens and fields, were never as popular here as in Europe. Thomas Jefferson acquired four thousand Hawthorns to enclose his orchards.

Today, on most historic sites only a fraction of the original landscape remains, and it is rare to have all of the above structures extant, not to mention the gardens and fields and bodies of water. However, one must remember that it was this total landscape that composed the settled Virginia countryside.

Summer Phlox and Crape Myrtle at SMITH'S FORT.

SMITH'S FORT PLANTATION (figures 1, 2). Foxglove (Digitalis purpurea) is one of several medicinal herbs growing at SMITH'S FORT PLANTATION (figure 3).

In 1609, Captain John Smith built a fort on this site for the protection of the colonists, hence the name. By 1614, Chief Powhatan had given this land to his daughter, Pocahontas, upon her marriage to John Rolfe. Records indicate that the present house was built by Thomas Warren at a much later date.

The garden is planted with appropriate seventeenth and eighteenth century perennial flowers and herbs (figure 2).

Overleaf, pages 64, 65: The use of Virginia rail, or worm, fences supposedly started in Virginia as an efficient way to use the byproducts of land clearing.

6

7

SCOTCHTOWN (c. 1719) (figure 5). Charles Chiswell built this fine house on 9,976 acres. The property was passed along to various members of the Chiswell family until John Payne, father of Dolley Payne Madison, became its owner. It was from John Payne that Patrick Henry purchased the house and 960 acres in 1771 and made it his home for the next seven years.

Rail fences define the tree-lined driveway entrance (figure 6).

Figure 7. A detail of one of the several wooden gates.

BURWELL-MORGAN MILL (1782). Originally this large stone mill was just one story high. The upper story was added later. Nathaniel Burwell, an enterprising planter from CARTER'S GROVE on the James River, combined forces with General Daniel Morgan to build and operate the mill. Morgan, after the Battle of Saratoga, was put in charge of Hessian prisoners camped near Winchester. It was these prisoners who allegedly built this massive stone structure (figure 9).

Appropriately, the grounds surrounding the mill have not been beautified by gardens and shrubs. Instead, natural features – water, rock ledges, large trees – were liberated from an overgrowth of wild shrubs, weeds, and vines so that they could be seen. Walking paths were added for the use of visitors while enjoying the beauties of the site.

The BURWELL-MORGAN MILL spillway swollen with spring rains (figure 8).

SMITHFIELD PLANTATION (1772). This plantation land was a crown grant to James Preston in 1745. He died in an Indian massacre ten years later. It was his nephew, Colonel William Preston, who built the present house which later became a Revolutionary War stronghold as well as the headquarters for the Preston family's land company in Virginia, West Virginia, and Kentucky.

Like SCOTCHTOWN, the house is distinguished by its architectural detail. It is situated on a rise of ground and commands a view in all directions across the surrounding fields (figure 13). These fields were divided into manageable parcels through the construction of fences. Hence, the prominence of fences in the landscape (figures 10, 12). When The Garden Club of Virginia restored the grounds in 1984, one of its goals was to display a collection of early frontier fence styles.

Every frontier plantation had to have a garden in which to grow the basic vegetables and herbs for human sustenance. It is not known precisely where the garden existed at SMITHFIELD. Archaeology did reveal the site of a smokehouse which has been reconstructed. The area between the main house and the smokehouse now contains a representative kitchen garden for demonstration purposes (figure 11). In this garden are grown typical crops such as beans, pumpkins, cabbages, lettuce, and carrots. A broad range of herbs – culinary, medicinal, and aromatic – are planted for educational purposes. Along the fence are raspberries, currants, and strawberries.

T wo of the better examples of the English landscape style outside of Britain are MONTICELLO and MOUNT VERNON. It was begun in the early eighteenth century by Charles Bridgeman, and was greatly advanced during the second quarter of the century by William Kent. It reached its zenith in the 1770's through its last great proponent, Lancelot "Capability" Brown.

What was the English landscape style, or the *jardin anglais* as it was called on the continent? It has been referred to as the "deformalization" of landscapes, where the main elements within the landscape became lawn, trees, and water all arranged in a "natural" manner. Others have said that it was the laying out of gardens "without level or line", referring to the system used to install the symmetrical or grid-plan gardens of the past.

It took more than half a century for the English landscape garden to reach North America. In 1785, after his return as leader of the Continental Army during the American Revolution, George Washington began to make major changes to his MOUNT VERNON estate. While he retained the two walled gardens (the lower garden to the south and the upper garden to the north of the mansion's entrance) he removed the walls on the west sides of each garden, and replaced them with a curved wall, thus changing the shape of the gardens to a shield rather than a simple rectangle. These alterations allowed him to change the form of the entrance drive and lawn between the two gardens. The results were a serpentine drive and a pear-shaped bowling green. Together these improvements produced a less formal landscape.

In addition, George Washington also installed ha-ha walls around the landscape surrounding the mansion. This allowed him to have uninterrupted views across his pastures and fields to the Potomac River and countryside outside the garden, and to see cattle and deer grazing in the middle distance. All of these alterations increased the pastoral quality of the landscape.

Thomas Jefferson had traveled extensively in both England and on the continent. He, too, chose to make the landscape at MONTICELLO in the "new style", but in the form of a *ferme ornée* or ornamental farm. Using this concept, even the vegetable garden was laid out with grass paths between each type of vegetable, the fields of grain were focal points in the landscape, and the tops of the fruit trees in the orchard provided a carpet of bloom beneath the view to distant mountains, when viewed from the terrace above. Roads and paths allowed visitors to walk throughout the farm and to view the gardens and fields, and to enjoy the shade of the grove. He planned to build a grotto and a water cascade for those walking through the landscape to enjoy.

While both of these important landscapes represent the *jardin anglais* in America, MOUNT VERNON is a more restrained version probably because George Washington was attempting to revise an already existing landscape. Thomas Jefferson, who through his readings and travels collected many ideas which he adapted to his mountain top, created the entire landscape himself without adapting an existing plan. Both gentlemen carefully consulted the dictates of the natural landscape – topography, water, soil conditions, vegetation, exposure – before making their plans for embellishment.

The cupola. MOUNT VERNON.

1

2

MOUNT VERNON (1735). George Washington acquired this estate in 1754, and it was his home until his death in 1799 except for the years of the Revolution and his presidency. Figure 1 shows the pear-shaped bowling green which was enclosed by a wide serpentine walk in 1785. On either side of this were planted informal groupings of trees which provide shade as well as enframement for this pleasant space.

Doves were common in eighteenth century landscapes, and several persist at MOUNT VERNON (figure 2).

In 1785, at the same time that the bowling green was constructed, the two walled gardens were enlarged and changed in shape from simple rectangles to shields by rounding off their northwest sides. The points of the shields were punctuated by small outbuildings (figure 3). The lower or vegetable garden was terraced in two levels. A pattern of walks divided each level into compartments, each one for a different kind of vegetable. The picket-fence-topped-brick wall also served as a support for espaliered fruit (figure 3).

In comparing the lower kitchen garden at MOUNT VERNON with the century earlier garden at BACON'S CASTLE, it is clear that an attempt was made to make MOUNT VERNON'S gardens more ornamental – a sign of the times. The detailing of the garden walls, the inclusion of the multi-sided garden buildings, the round-

ing of the garden ends, the addition of geometrically shaped cisterns, and the varied shapes for the garden compartments, are all indicative of a conscious effort to ornament.

The orangery was destroyed by fire in 1835 and was later constructed. It sits on the upper or north side of the flower garden and is flanked by slave quarters on either side (figure 4). Plots in the flower garden are of varied shapes and sizes and the intervening walks allow visitors to study the variety of flowers and shrubs. At the rounded end of this garden is the schoolhouse (figure 5).

All sections of the lawn surrounding the mansion are separated from the surrounding fields by a ha-ha wall so as not to interrupt the continuous view to the Potomac River and the distant countryside (figure 6).

MONTICELLO (1768). Thomas Jefferson named his estate MONTICELLO, or little mountain, since it is surrounded by higher elevations. The views from there are spectacular (figure 8).

The West Lawn at MONTICELLO is enclosed by a serpentine walk and along this walk are flower beds where Mr. Jefferson grew and studied various species of flowers (figure 7). On the outer edge of the Lawn was his eighteen-acre grove which was restored by The Thomas Jefferson Memorial Foundation in 1978 (figures 8, 9).

11

Previous pages, 78, 79: The traditional view of MONTICELLO looking across the West Lawn, the round-about walk, and spring tulips. Thomas Jefferson began his vegetable garden on the south slope of MONTICELLO in 1770. There he grew vegetables in contoured rows. In 1806 he started terracing the slope to create a relatively flat vegetable garden of one thousand feet in length. This garden overlooked a large apple orchard and vineyard. All of these important features were restored in the early 1980's (figure 11).

This large terrace garden was arranged with grass walks around twenty-four plots, or squares. In each square was grown a different category of vegetable – leaves, roots, and fruits (such as lettuce, beets, or beans). At the outer edge of the garden was Jefferson's twelve-and-one-half feet square garden pavilion in which he could sit, admire the orderly garden, and look out over the top of his orchard and vineyard to the mountains beyond (figure 11).

Scarlet Runner Beans and Savoy Cabbages were two favorites of Mr. Jefferson (figures 12, 13).

12

The colonial revival movement began following the Great Centennial Exhibition, in Philadelphia, in 1876. After this one hundredth birthday of our nation there was a strong patriotic spirit for "being American". It was expressed in architecture and landscape architecture by the inclusion of elements from the colonial past.

What does colonial revival mean? Basically, it is the revival of plans and features thought to be colonial, as idealized through the eyes and mind of a later time. It is the design of gardens thought to be appropriate to a site but not based on actual research. It has been said that colonial revival gardens were designed to "give the beholders what they expected to see" rather than what actually had existed.

As a garden design period, the colonial revival continues to this day especially in reproduction architecture and associated landscapes. Sometimes it is used on historic sites when data are lacking, though the trend is away from this practice.

Virginia is rich in colonial revival style. Many of the gardens at Colonial Williamsburg are of that period. These are the gardens with broad, sweeping masses of evergreen groundcovers, or those with raised beds made of modern, sawed planking. These are the gardens with intricate parterres, and sundials at cross-walks, neither of which is based on actual fact.

The colonial revival was at its height in the 1920's and 1930's. There was a reluctance to show landscapes as they actually would have been for fear that they would offend the aesthetic eye of the viewers. To this day many administrators of eighteenth century historic sites are concerned when

their gardens do not display bloom throughout the growing season, even though this is a concept of the late nineteenth and twentieth centuries.

Arthur Schurcliff, Williamsburg's first landscape architect, was a practitioner of the colonial revival. He also designed the restorations for The Garden Club of Virginia at STARTFORD HALL, SMITH'S FORT, WILTON, AND BRUTON PARISH CHURCH. His successor, Alden Hopkins, carried on the colonial revival concept at GUNSTON HALL, and the ADAM THOROUGHGOOD HOUSE. Charles F. Gillatee designed a colonial revival garden at KENMORE. All of these gardens became models for gardens to be created throughout the country.

Today, with perfected research skills and advanced technology, it is easier, though costly, to obtain historical documentation. Garden archaeology has advanced greatly since the first gardens were excavated in the 1920's and thus provides an authoritative source for historical documentation (see BACON'S CASTLE, page 15). Other techniques, such as aerial photogrammetry, dendrochronology, and carbon dating, provide planners with hard basic data on which to base their restoration decisions.

It is unlikely that we will see many more landscapes created in the colonial revival style except on private estates. Perhaps this behooves us to preserve those that were created during the last century as examples of this vanishing art form.

The GOVERNOR'S PALACE garden, Colonial Williamsburg.

LIGHTFOOT TENEMENT HOUSE,
WILLIAMSBURG. A simple symmetrical garden of the eighteenth century
expressed in the colonial revival manner
(figure 1).

An ancient Paper Mulberry (Broussonetia papyrifera) is the focus of
this colonial revival garden at the
ORLANDO JONES HOUSE, Williamsburg (figure 2).

3

CARLYLE HOUSE (1752). Two companion brick buildings that once flanked either side of this fine house were removed in the last century. An old engraving shows the front lawn treated very simply with just two Red Cedars (Juniperus virginiana) on either side of the main walk (figure 3). When the Scottish merchant, John Carlyle, built this house on an acre lot it overlooked the Potomac River. Over the years land was filled and the shoreline pushed away from the vicinity of the house. The existing garden was installed in recent years by The Northern Virginia Park Authority, owners of the property (figure 4).

4

MARY WASHINGTON HOUSE (before 1772) (figures 5, 6, 7). George Washington purchased this house for his mother in 1772. According to legend, she planted boxwood that still grows on either side of the walk which she walked to visit her daughter, Betty Lewis, at nearby KENMORE (figure 7). No other evidence of the original garden remains.

In August, the sculptural Crape Myrtle (Lagerstroemia indica), embowers the walk in a canopy of pink bloom (figure 7).

The nineteenth century saw a broad range of landscape treatments from the simple tree groves surrounding southern residences to complex eclectic schemes during the late Victorian period. In the early part of the nineteenth century, many adopted the English landscape style for their general landscape, while retaining the traditional grid plan for their gardens.

Legend has it that Thomas Jefferson assisted several fellow Virginians in laying out their houses and grounds. For example, it is alleged that he designed BELLE GROVE for his friend James Madison's sister, Eleanor Conway Madison, wife of Major Isaac Hite, Jr. Since Jefferson was a strong proponent of groves as protection from the hot summer sun, it is quite likely that he also suggested the grove idea for BELLE GROVE.

It is said that Thomas Jefferson also advised George Carter on the design of the north wall at OATLANDS. Jefferson had traveled beyond the boundaries of France when he was United States Minister to France between 1785 and 1790. He observed the practice of capping walls with wood, thatch, and sod as a means for preserving them. At MONTICELLO he later built a sod capped wall to retain the garden terrace, and it is quite likely that he suggested the wood capped wall for OATLANDS.

As the nineteenth century progressed, citizens became increasingly interested in our history and heritage as well as that of the rest of the world. More people traveled to, or read about, distant lands. New ideas were incorporated into the landscape and thus was born the eclectic period where a single landscape would have several garden styles within its confines. As an example, MAYMONT had a large Italian garden, an even larger Japanese garden, an extensive and rolling English lawn, as well as several sculptural features placed about the landscape.

Earlier in the nineteenth century, boxwood parterres and knot gardens had a strong revival, apparently part of a larger movement that concerned itself with geometric detail in both house and garden design. Boxwood edging has since become a symbol of Virginia gardens. In the eighteenth century, single plants of boxwood were used as accents in the garden. For example, in Lady Jean Skipwith's garden at PRESTWOULD (see pages 34-39), specimens of boxwood were planted on either side of the garden entrances, as well as at the corners of some of the garden quadrants, a plan not unique to PRESTWOULD.

During the nineteenth century technological advances fostered the mass production of garden furnishings such as lamp posts, benches, sculptures, urns, gazebos, and even bird houses, mostly of cast iron. The dogs that sit on the wings of the main steps at CENTER HILL, and in the garden at OATLANDS are fine examples of this craft.

The nineteenth century began with essentially two landscape styles – the traditional and symmetrical grid plan, and the new English landscape style (see page 72). As the century drew to a close, many styles were represented in one garden or separately in several small gardens.

Pastoral setting. BELLE GROVE.

BELLE GROVE (1794). Major Isaac Hite, Jr., grandson of the first named settler in the Shenandoah Valley, built this house for his wife, Eleanor Conway Madison, sister of James Madison, our fourth president. It is hard to realize that the peaceful, rolling fields surrounding BELLE GROVE were the site of the Battle of Cedar Creek during the Civil War (figure 1).

Today the landscape surrounding BELLE GROVE consists primarily of trees which tower over the house in keeping with past tradition. A large cutting and herb garden supplies plant material for decoration and educational demonstrations (figure 2).

OATLANDS (1803). The garden is a series of terraces, the largest of which surrounds the mansion and is bounded by a balustrade in the Italian Renaissance style (figure 4). Various garden styles contribute to the total landscape at OATLANDS such as the reflecting pool (figure 5), and a wood-roofed, stepped garden forcing wall (figure 6).

Figure 3. The main steps in the extensive terraced garden at OATLANDS ascend to the large balustraded terrace surrounding the mansion.

Overleaf, pages 90, 91: These garden dependencies at OATLANDS sheltered the many domestic services.

7

8

9

The present configuration of the OATLANDS garden is attributed to George Carter, the original builder. Many of the eclectic and enriching details throughout the garden were added by Mrs. William Corcoran Eustis, the third owner, following 1903 (figures 8, 9). From the mansion, sited on the highest terrace, there are impressive vistas over the garden and rolling fields to the mountains beyond (figure 7).

The foundation of the mansion at OATLANDS is properly bare of plantings as it would have been in the decades following its construction (figure 10).

10

CENTER HILL (c. 1820). Robert Bolling IV built this Federal style house on a nineteen-acre site (figure 11). By the mid-nineteenth century, about half of the estate was a collection of trees and shrubs, both evergreen and deciduous. A large vegetable and fruit garden, a tree nursery, an orangery, stables, and servants quarters were sited on a terrace below the house to the east.

These two cast iron dogs were not part of the original architecture but they have guarded the entrance for over one hundred years (figure 12).

POINT OF HONOR (c. 1815). Overlooking the James River, this Federal style house was built by Dr. James E. Cabell, Sr., an eminent physician. As with many houses of this period, it is assumed that POINT OF HONOR has always been sheltered by a tree grove much as it is today (figure 13). In the absence of documentation concerning the past landscape, the grounds have been restored simply. A stone forecourt was installed, and the boundary walls and gates rebuilt in the nineteenth century manner. The interior of the house displays intricate architectural detail. Here a basket-vase filled with flowers repeats a similar one in the Federal style wallpaper (figure 14).

KENT-VALENTINE HOUSE (1845). Mr. Horace Kent had this house built from plans drawn by the Boston architect Isaiah Rogers. The house was purchased by Mr. Granville G. Valentine in 1904. It became The Garden Club of Virginia's headquarters in 1971. The property, a small city lot, is rich in original cast iron. The porch rails were saved from a previous porch. Fences and gates remain intact. Two large cast iron urns, suitable to the architecture, accent the inviting front entrance (figures 16, 17).

Figure 15. The classical revival portico of the KENT-VALENTINE HOUSE, headquarters of The Garden Club of Virginia.

Several Southern Magnolias (Magnolia grandiflora), and a large Hackberry (Celtis occidentalis) shade the grounds.

18

Figure 18. The portico of the WOODROW WILSON BIRTHPLACE, STAUNTON, VIRGINIA (1845) in spring splendor.

Thomas Woodrow Wilson, twenty-eighth president of the United States, was born in the Manse in 1856 when his father was pastor of the First Presbyterian Church. At the time of his birth there were outbuildings standing on the site of the present bow-knot garden, planted by The Garden Club of Virginia in 1933 (figure 19). The inspiration for this design came from a plan that was drawn by a resident of the Manse after the Wilsons. The plan was discovered by landscape architect, Charles F. Gillette, while conducting research for the garden. It is not known if the plan had been executed previously.

Summer visitors to the Manse are welcomed by this Victorian wire planter filled with geraniums (figure 20).

MAYMONT (1893). Major James Dooley and his wife, Sallie May, created MAYMONT in the eclectic style. An old Atlas Cedar (Cedrus atlantica glauca) shades one of several gazebos on the estate (figure 21). MAYMONT'S Japanese garden is attributed to Muto, the designer of several well-known gardens in Philadelphia. This extensive garden lies at the base of a waterfall. A moon bridge spans the stream that winds through the garden (figure 23).

Beneath the ramparts of the Italian Garden (see overleaf) emerges a water-step cascade, a feature often associated with such gardens. Its water source emerges from the lion's head (figure 22).

Overleaf, pages 102, 103: The Italian Garden at MAYMONT with handsome, twisted Wisteria stems (Wisteria sinensis) growing upon the pergola.

22

CHIPPOKES (1854) (figure 25). A long allee of stately Red Cedars (Juniperus virginiana) borders one side of the garden. The diameter of their trunks suggests that these trees date from the nineteenth century (figure 24).

The garden, a remnant of a larger one that was designed in the traditional, symmetrical plan, flourishes today with modern cultivars of azaleas (figures 25, 26).

In 1967, Mrs. Victor Stewart gave CHIPPOKES to the Commonwealth of Virginia, and it is now a State Park for all to enjoy.

By the early twentieth century the dominant garden styles in this country were colonial revival, Italian, domestic English, Spanish, and the naturalistic Japanese, according to a

1905 article in COUNTRY LIFE IN AMERICA. While this statement appears to be true, one should not overlook the vernacular garden which is based on the cultural background of the creator. Eclectic gardens were also made well into the twentieth century, but each garden type lost its definite edges and blended better into the whole within a given landscape.

In Virginia, especially in the Windsor Farms section of Richmond, there was great interest in the English domestic garden. This term referred to a garden with a distinct entrance forecourt from which access could be gained to both the residence and its service quarters. The major living spaces of the house overlooked the most favorable aspects of the landscape, usually a series of walled or hedged gardens, and if the site permitted, distant views beyond. Within the various gardens were features reminiscent of English Tudor or cottage gardens.

The sunken pond garden at HAMPTON COURT became a prototype for many gardens in this country. In fact, to many people the term "English garden" came to mean a sunken garden rather than a garden of the natural style described on page 72.

AGECROFT and VIRGINIA HOUSE are two excellent examples of the English domestic garden as interpreted in the early twentieth century. Their walled and hedged private spaces, the changes in levels, their sunken gardens, all of which were highlighted by features such as water, sculpture, and appropriate plantings, were brilliantly articulated by landscape architect Charles

F. Gillette.

As in most English domestic gardens, the influence of Gertrude Jekyll, the great English garden designer, and her associate, architect Edwin Lutyens, can readily be seen. Jekyll's concern for color and texture, sequence of bloom and rythmic massing, have strongly affected the way gardens have been designed to this day. The heavy and detailed use of stone and brick for walls, steps, and pavement, as well as other architectonic features, were brought to garden design by Lutyens whose ideas greatly affected the appearance of American garden design in the first half of the twentieth century.

Both Jekyll and Lutyens drew their inspiration for their garden designs from the cottage gardens of Surrey, Sessex, West Sussex, and adjoining counties in England. They observed details in paving, walls, steps, and architecture, improved upon them, and used them in their garden plans on a grander scale than the original cottage gardens. In so doing, they were adapting the vernacular to their new schemes.

Not all gardens, however, were influenced by these popular styles. The vernacular garden of ANNE SPENCER has been called a "cottage type" garden. This is because she arranged her plants in a highly informal manner within a structured plan that expressed her life-style and her interests. It was a highly personal garden, each detail evolving from her ethnic past as well as from the knowledge she acquired through life. The garden ANNE SPENCER created served as an inspiration for most of her poetical works.

A wistful, watchful, lion. MONTPELIER.

AGECROFT (English Tudor, moved from England and reconstructed in Richmond in 1926). Landscape architect, Charles Gillette, was commissioned to design the grounds for AGECROFT HALL by its owners, Mr. and Mrs. Thomas C. Williams, Jr. He included as many features associated with English manor houses as were appropriate to the site. One of these was the sunken garden featuring a circular pool in the center with perennial borders on raised terraces on the sides and ends (figure 1). The central focus on the upper terrace is a statue of Pan (figures 1, 3).

A Tudor knot and parterre garden on three levels was installed, east of the manor house, to provide herbs, flowers, and vegetables for the household.

Figure 1. The sunken garden at AGECROFT reminiscent of the Pond Garden at HAMPTON COURT, in England.

VIRGINIA HOUSE (English Twelfth Century, moved to Richmond and reconstructed in 1925). This house was built in part from ancient Warwick Priory by Mr. and Mrs. Alexander Weddell. Because the terrain sloped sharply from the house to the James River, the landscape architect, Charles F. Gillette, designed a series of terraces (figures 4, 5). These, called "The Pleasances", set the stage for several artful gardens, and the walls provided suitable places on which to display an array of sculpture (figures 4, 5). From these terraces, vistas were cut through the trees to the River, thus borrowing from the distant landscape. Gillette employed an ancient Persian device in the Water Garden, a narrow channel of water, called a "rill", connecting two pools (figure 5). Rills were revived by the famous British architect, Edwin Lutyens, and his associate, the garden designer Gertrude Jekyll. American landscape architects included rills in many American gardens from coast to coast in the late 1920's and 1930's.

The many balustrades and balconies at VIRGINIA HOUSE provided ideal places to grow vines such as this Wisteria (Wisteria sinensis), a plant imported from China in 1816 (figure 7).

5

6

7

MONTPELIER (1760). Very little is known about the original garden at MONTPELIER, the home of James Madison and his father before him. It is believed that Madison created the terraces we now see in the garden, though they have been changed over the years. The grounds surrounding the house were park-like during Madison's life, as they are today, with large specimen trees in the lawn (figure 8). President Madison's ice-house, a circular structure deep in the ground with a classical "tempietto" on top, is original to his period of ownership (figure 10).

After Dolley Madison sold the property in 1844 there was a succession of owners. In 1901, Mr. and Mrs. William duPont purchased the estate. In the decade follow-ing, rehabilitation of the five-acre enclosed garden began. Mrs. duPont noted: "It had a Virginia worm fence across the foot of the garden and a paling fence on the other three sides . . . The only path was the earth incline path from the entrance to the foot of the garden. The box hedge was broken and bare at the bottom and over-grown on top . . . and [the] small terraces had been ploughed down . . . It took 22 years to get the box in

present shape. All the plantings of trees, shrubs and flowers are my design."

In 1989, The Garden Club of Virginia agreed to restore the garden to the era of Mrs. William duPont and her daughter, Marion duPont Scott, who inherited the garden in 1928. Fortunately, much documentation existed. Photographs showed that Mrs. duPont had removed the fences and installed a high, English type brick wall (figure 9). The worn down terraces had been rebuilt and steps and walks had been added. The duPont's had installed planting beds – roses for the top terraces, crescent shaped perennial beds for the next terraces (see overleaf), parterre beds of annuals at the next lower level, and beds of lilies and annuals on the bottom terrace. Throughout the garden were shrubs and trees for background and accent.

Many pieces of sculpture were imported from abroad. A detail from one of the largest vases from the top ter-race is shown in figure 11.

Overleaf, pages 112, 113: Two large crescent beds adorn the second highest garden terrace at MONTPELIER.

ANNE SPENCER'S GARDEN (c. 1905). For over seventy years the prominent Harlem Renaissance poet, Anne Spencer, with the help of her husband Edward, created and tended her cottage-type garden. In plan it was long and linear with flower beds along the walk and vine covered arbors for resting along the way. A rose covered trellis (figure 14) made a sweet and welcoming entrance for their visitors, well known to all including Rev. Martin Luther King, Jr., James Weldon Johnson, George Washington Carver, and Marian Anderson. A frequent guest was W.E.B. DuBois, who gave Anne Spencer the cast iron head of "Prince Ebo", which she had affixed to the rim of their pool in the rear section of the garden (figure 15).

Figure 13. EVELYNTON (Eighteenth Century, rebuilt in 1932). The colonial revival rose arbor and boxwood garden.

Overleaf, pages 116, 117: BLOEMENDAAL (c. 1885). The Grace E. Arents garden in the springtime, now part of the Lewis Ginter Botanical garden.

Two popular components of the GLEN BURNIE landscape are the Chinese Garden and the Water Garden (figures 18, 20, and overleaf). In addition, there are two rose gardens, a sculpture garden, a cutting garden, and a formal vegetable garden. All of these were created by Mr. Julian Glass with the assistance of his friend, Mr. Lee Taylor. GLEN BURNIE is on the site of Colonel James Wood's house (1750) and grounds. Woods was the founder of Winchester.

Figure 17. GLEN BURNIE (c. 1750). The Pink Palladian Pavilion, with its bust of Hadrian over the door, is situated in a boxwood parterre garden.

A mantle of ivy is maintained on the head of "Hadrian's Mother" (figure 19).

Overleaf, pages 120, 121: The Chinese Garden at GLEN BURNIE, complete with moon bridge and tea house.

The nineteenth century has been referred to as the "golden era of horticulture." As technology advanced, the work week was shortened and more time was released for leisure, thus encouraging the creation of gardens and public spaces for recreation. New and exotic plants were introduced from all parts of the world; garden features were mass produced from cast iron, wood, and stone; books on various horticultural subjects were printed; and machinery to aid the gardener, such as the lawn mower, was advanced.

In 1825 a movement began that led to the great rural cemetery era. Dr. Jacob Bigelow, a resident of Boston, formed a committee to plan and purchase land in Cambridge for a burial place to be laid out in a manner quite different from the traditional graveyards. The impetus for such a scheme was a concern for greater sanitation in the way people were buried, as well as the desire to provide a more attractive setting for the burial place. The plan which evolved for Mt. Auburn Cemetery by 1830, was sensitive to the land. Roads and paths followed the contours, marshy places were

made into ponds and lakes, a belvedere was built on the highest summit, and the entire acerage was planted with a vast collection of ornamental trees and shrubs. In short, the cemetery became quite park-like.

The concept of rural cemeteries, as they were called, took hold rapidly. In 1847, Joshua Jefferson Fry and William Henry Haxall started a drive to establish HOLLYWOOD CEMETERY in Richmond. Similar cemeteries were established throughout the country. Mourners, as well as others with no interest in the dead, found these rural cemeteries pleasant places to visit during leisure time. It was not long after the establishment of Mt. Auburn Cemetery that the great horticultur-

ist, Andrew Jackson Downing, wrote: "But does not this great general interest [in landscaped spaces] manifested in these cemeteries, prove that public gardens, established in liberal and suitable manner, near large cities, would be equally successful?" It was not long afterwards, in 1853, that the great public park movement started in America.

Prior to rural cemeteries, burials took place in church yards or private burial plots on each plantation or farm. These plots, where graves were row-on-row, are important features in the Virginia landscape. Many of the earlier ones, such as BRUTON PARISH CHURCHYARD, and CHRIST CHURCH LANCASTER, are enclosed with fine brick walls. In the nineteenth century, cast iron was used as boundary fencing and to delineate burial plots within the churchyard. Grave markers, flower urns and vases, and benches were also made of cast iron.

As the new rural cemeteries and public parks were developed throughout Virginia and the rest of the nation, exotic as well as native trees, shrubs, and flowers were planted to enhance the grounds. Trees shaded the paths and drives, as well as certain of the burial plots, while shrubs enriched the boundaries of the various spaces and provided color throughout the season. Flower beds accented the entrances and brightened the paths.

Throughout the South, churchyards are repositories for old shrub roses. Over the years mourners planted the ever popular rose at the heads of graves or along fences. Today some of the finest old rose collections are in these graveyards.

Tombstone detail. BRUTON PARISH CHURCH, Williamsburg.

BRUTON PARISH CHURCH (1715) (figure 3). This impressive structure, the third built on the site of the original 1660 church, was designed by Lieutenant Governor Alexander Spotswood. The churchyard was surrounded by a high brick wall built according to Samuel Spurr's plans in 1745, and restored in the 1930's (figure 1). Trees shade the graves, and old roses and other flowering shrubs grow along the walls (figure 2). While it is a favorite visitors' stop in Williamsburg, the church has not lost its dignity as a house of worship. It is thought to be the oldest Episcopal Church in the country in continuous worship.

4

Figure 4. CHRIST CHURCH, LANCASTER (1732). Simply landscaped grounds allow this elegant church to remain constantly in focus and the primary feature in the landscape.

A high brick wall encloses the original churchyard (figure 6). In 1732, Robert "King" Carter, a prominent planter and government official, built CHRIST CHURCH at his own expense. His tomb, an excellent example of the art, is in the churchyard (overleaf, pages 126, 127).

The West Entrance of the church (figure 5) is aligned with a "row of goodly Cedars", a portion of which was restored in 1968. The Cedars (Juniperus virginiana) are suggestive of the three mile allee that once connected the church with Mr. Carter's plantation on the Corotoman River.

CHRIST CHURCH, FINCASTLE (1770). After 1838 and throughout the nineteenth century, cast iron replaced brick as an inexpensive way to enclose churchyards and family burial plots.

LEE CHAPEL, WASHINGTON AND LEE UNIVERSITY (1867). This Victorian chapel of great beauty and dignity was built during the college presidency of Robert E. Lee. When he died in 1870 his funeral was held in this chapel, and he was later laid to rest in the crypt beneath the church.

MARY WASHINGTON MONUMENT (1893). The period from the end of the Civil War to the start of the great depression may be characterized, among other things, as the era of monuments. They were built to commemorate soldiers or generals, doctors and clergymen, politicians and inventors, or any other person of note. The MARY WASHINGTON MONUMENT, was built to mark the grave of the mother of George Washington, who had resided a short distance away. In 1937, The Garden Club of Virginia constructed the wall around the cemetery and built steps from the street. At that time, tree and shrubs plantings were installed, and many more have been added in recent years (figure 10).

Prior to the last years of the nineteenth century, public buildings and college campuses were landscaped only with trees. The practice of encircling each building with foundation

plantings had not yet begun. At colleges and universities to be sure, there were enclosed gardens for pleasure and study, but the basic campus landscape treatment was largely trees and grass. Old pictures taken in the late nineteenth century of the present VIRGINIA UNION UNIVERSITY show the campus devoid of foundation plantings but plentiful with trees, shading the walks and buildings, and with specimen trees in the lawn. A careful study of these pictures shows trees regularly spaced along most of the sidewalks and driveways. It was unfortunate that such plantings utilized just a few species – Maples, Oaks, Ash, Elms – thus creating a virtual monoculture which became vulnerable to attack by diseases and insects resulting in their early demise.

This type of landscape treatment prevailed on the grounds of most institutions – colleges, hospitals, courthouses, churches, private schools – throughout the country.

Foundation plantings became popular in the last decade of the nineteenth century. By that time, the palette of shrubs had increased through plant explorations and introductions. Such plants as Cutleaf Maples, False Cypress, and a wide range of Japanese Yews and Chinese Junipers, were standard components of foundation plantings. Deciduous plants – Hydrangeas, Spireas, Forsythias, Chaenomeles – offered desirable flowers and interesting foliage throughout the growing season.

Thomas Jefferson planned the UNIVERSITY OF VIRGINIA in about 1816. Although the LAWN in front of the Rotunda was rich architecturally,

with ten pavilions exhibiting the five Roman orders, the plantings were simple. They consisted of a row of trees on either side of the LAWN. There were no shrubs or small trees.

Mr. Jefferson drew a plan to show the arrangement for gardens behind each pavilion. While he indicated an enclosed garden space for each, he did not leave details for the plantings. Perhaps he intended that each pavilion inhabitant develop his own garden. In alternate gardens on each side of the LAWN, the lower compartment was set off by a serpentine brick wall. This part of the garden was to be for the production of fruits and vegetables to supply the cafeterias, or hotels, as they were called.

College campuses, through their extensive plantings of trees, became virtual arboreta. From the late eighteenth century, and especially through the nineteenth, as plants were introduced from all over the world, what better places were there than seats of learning to start collections?

Virginia is fortunate to have several botanical gardens and arboreta within its boundaries. Her diverse climate, from the Tidewater to the Blue Ridge Mountains, offers a wide range of conditions, similar to the range from Mississippi to southern Maine. At these public gardens, plants may be studied and collections of them are displayed for the education and enjoyment of all. Botanical gardens, like arboreta, specialize in plants suitable to their region. At the NORFOLK BOTANICAL GARDEN there are major displays of azaleas, roses, and camellias.

New Scholar Trees (Sophora japonica). VIRGINIA UNION UNIVERSITY.

3

UNIVERSITY OF VIRGINIA (1817). The center of Thomas Jefferson's academical village consists of the magnificent Rotunda, originally the library, at the head of a long lawn panel. On either side of The Lawn are five pavilions, connected one to the other with a series of dormitory rooms. Colonnades provide shelter from the sun and rain (figure 2). Behind these buildings, on both the east and west sides, are the pavilion gardens, ten in all. According to Peter Maverick's 1822 plan of the academical village, each garden was enclosed by a high wall, part of which is Jefferson's original serpentine wall (figure 3). In alternate gardens were dividing walls creating two separate garden spaces. The one nearest the pavilion was probably intended for the pleasure of the professor and his family who lived within. The other is said to have been a kitchen garden to supply the student "hotels", or cafeterias.

Figure 1. PAVILION VIII, UNIVERSITY OF VIRGINIA. A gravel walk, surrounding a lawn panel laid out in the form of an hour glass, is the center of this spring and early summer garden.

THE COLONNADE CLUB (1817). This is a private faculty club and the oldest building at the UNIVERSITY OF VIRGINIA. The inspiration for the garden's circular design came from LeRouge's JARDIN ANGLO-CHINOIS (1785). Alden Hopkins, who master planned the restoration, based his design decisions on existing site conditions and examples from eighteenth and nineteenth century texts (figure 4).

When The Garden Club of Virginia decided in 1948 to undertake the restoration of the ten gardens, they began work on the west side. Work was completed in 1952. Eight years elapsed before the east gardens were restored. They were more complicated and costly to restore because a road, with adjoining parking, had been installed across the five gardens, thus destroying most of the serpentine walls as well as other parts of the gardens. As a result, the east gardens were completed in 1965.

Mr. Alden Hopkins, the landscape architect, drew a conceptual plan for all ten gardens with working drawings for those to be restored first. In 1960, just before work was to begin on the east gardens, Mr. Hopkins died. His successor, Mr. Donald Parker completed the work.

5

6

PAVILION V. The design for this garden – a central panel surrounded by a hedge and four circles of boxwood – was inspired by an example that Alden Hopkins found in John Claudius Loudon's ENCYCLOPEDIA OF GARDENING (LONDON, 1822) (figure 5).

The plants used in the restoration of the Pavilion Gardens are all authentic to the early nineteenth century and before. Prominent in figure 6 are the blue Chaste Tree (Vitex agnuscastus), introduced in 1750, and a Weeping Willow (Salix babylonica), 1730.

8

NORFOLK BOTANICAL GARDEN (1938). As part of a Works Progress Administration (WPA) project, about two hundred women worked to clear overgrowth from the old Azalea Garden By the Sea and to lay the groundwork for what was to become the NORFOLK BOTANICAL GARDEN.

In the Renaissance Garden pool is a row of impressive bronze lions of popular interest to visitors (figure 7). This garden is famous for its dogwoods, azaleas, and rhododendrons, as well as other members of the genus Rhododendron. Some are displayed in informal masses naturalistically planted along paths or roadsides. Others take on a more formal arrangement such as those in the Sunken Garden (figure 8).

THE NORFOLK BOTANICAL GARDEN has a sequence of bloom throughout the season. In addition to the ericaceous plants and dogwoods, and a large rose garden, there are masses of Oleanders (Nerium oleander), and a Mimosa Tree (Albizzia julibrissin) over-hanging one of the streams (figure 9).

Overleaf, pages 138, 139: There are many pools and other bodies of water in the NORFOLK BOTANICAL GARDEN, as well as fine sculpture. Here water and sculpture combine with Two Dancing Maidens in Friendship Pond.

11

CHRYSLER MUSEUM (1933). This MUSEUM was originally called The Norfolk Museum for the Arts and
Sciences. Mr. Walter Chrysler, Jr. gave a major portion
of his art collection to Norfolk in 1971. In appreciation
the MUSEUM was renamed in his honor.

In 1989 extensive renovations were made to the
MUSEUM which partially destroyed the Memorial Garden. As soon as construction ended, the Garden was
restored, using the original plans by landscape architect,
Peter Rowland, with some modifications. The Garden
Club of Norfolk was responsible for the restoration and
has overseen its maintenance (figures 11, 12).

Figure 12. During the summer Hydrangeas (Hydran-
gea macrophylla) complement the refreshing pool and
fountain.

PORTSMOUTH COURTHOUSE (1846). This fine
example of courthouse architecture is now being used
as a cultural center for the City of Portsmouth. The
yard surrounding it provides ample space for outdoor
activities. Plantings along its iron fence, though not
authentic to the nineteenth century, provide screen-
ing and noise abatement from the heavy traffic of
today.

Previous pages, 142, 143: THE MEWS (1967). A detail
of a section of cast iron that was incorporated into
the wall surrounding THE MEWS, Church Hill, Richmond. The MEWS are a garden-park in the center of
the Pilot Block, a restored group of row houses. THE
MEWS were created along an old and original alley.
The garden is shaded by overhanging trees, and the
main feature in the garden is a pavilion in which visitors may sit and enjoy the daffodils and azaleas that
bloom each spring.